# AN ODE TO THE OCEAN IN MY HEART

Jordan Asbroek

First published by Busybird Publishing 2024

Copyright © 2024 Jordan Asbroek

**ISBN:** 978-1-923216-68-6

This book is copyright. Apart from any fair dealing for the purposes of study, research, criticism, review, or as otherwise permitted under the Copyright Act, no part may be reproduced by any process without written permission. Enquiries should be made through the publisher.

This is a work of fiction. Any similarities between places and characters are a coincidence.

**Cover image:** @melissabrown_photographer

**Cover design:** Busybird Publishing

**Layout and typesetting:** Busybird Publishing

Busybird Publishing
2/118 Para Road
Montmorency, Victoria
Australia 3094
www.busybird.com.au

# DEDICATION

For those who find solace in
the written word,
who see the world through
the lens of possibility,
and who embrace the journey
of discovery.
This book is for you.
And to the ocean in my heart,
a boundless expanse of my
wildly adventurous mind.
Its depths have fuelled my
dreams,
its waves have carried my
thoughts,
and its serenity has calmed
my spirit.
This is an ode to the endless
blue within me,
forever guiding my hand to
put pen to paper.

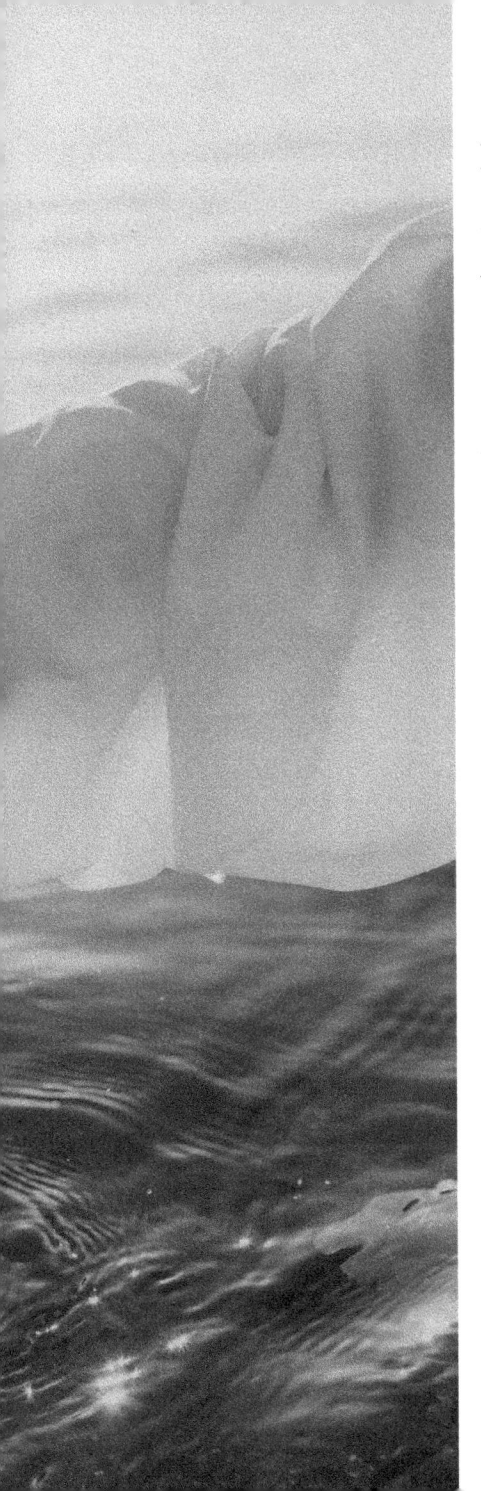

# BOOK SYNOPSIS

In *"An Ode To The Ocean In My Heart,"* I lay bare my soul, sharing the innermost depths of my being with raw honesty. It's about living with mental health struggles, navigating the maze of trauma as a young woman in a world that can feel merciless.

I delve into the darkest corners of my mind, revealing the turmoil of my thoughts and emotions. Through my words, I offer a glimpse into the challenges I face and the battles I fight every day.

But amidst the darkness, there's a glimmer of hope—a hope that by sharing my story, I can reach out to others who may be struggling too. I want my words to be a source of comfort and understanding, a reminder that no one is alone in their journey.

*"An Ode To The Ocean In My Heart"* is more than just a memoir; it's a testament to resilience, a testament to the strength we all possess to overcome the toughest of obstacles. And I hope that by sharing my story, I can help others find their own path to healing and self-acceptance.

# Contents

THE PAIN                1

THE REFLECTION         43

THE LOVE               63

THE HEALING            97

THE GROWING           123

ABOUT THE AUTHOR      153

# THE PAIN

# FADING FAREWELL

in the silence of the room

i remember the words that were left unsaid

the pain of our parting

echoes in my heart like a relentless drumbeat

you deserved a kinder goodbye

one filled with love and understanding

not the harsh words that hung in the air

like a heavy fog

suffocating us both

i wish i could turn back time

and rewrite our final moments

but all i can do now is carry the weight of regret

and hope that someday

you'll forgive me

i will hold onto the memories we shared

and the love that once filled our hearts

but i will always carry the guilt of knowing

that you deserved a kinder goodbye

## BUILDING BRIDGES, NOT BARRIERS

conversations should bridge hearts

not divide

feelings shared

understood

should not be lost in an argument

## THREE FLAMES

they say bad things come in threes

and this is true with you

you showed me how to start a fire

how easy it is to ignite someone who loves you

now you stand back

watching

doing nothing as they burn

## **WHISPERS OF THE NIGHT**

some nights i cry so hard

that my body aches

i shake

and i have to hold my mouth shut

so no one can hear the breathless screams

there are nights where i'm happy

i'm happy that you're happy

and it leaves me wondering

if i can only feel happiness in others

then there are nights where i feel nothing at all

i am numb

i am cold

but there is never a night

where you don't cross my mind

and i hope you're sleeping soundly

sleep tight

good night

# CHAOS AND CALM

inconsistent as spring's wild weather

i roar with thunder

pour out rain

then suddenly

stillness takes over

gathering myself with what remains

with the last bit of sun

i'll shine to make you see

it was just a scattered day

spring has sprung again

## SHOWERS

some days

my mind is overflowing

thoughts surging like tides

unrelenting

leaving no room for air

i can't even shower

the thought of it

the act of standing

breathing

feels too heavy

my body

frozen and aching

every muscle weighed down

as if moving might shatter me

the warm water pours over me

a steady stream

and all i feel is drowning

pulled under

by the invisible weight

of my own mind

## ODE TO HEALING

i wish the memories from that night would leave me

the echoes of pain

haunting endlessly

when you forced yourself upon me

you broke much more than my pride

you created a wound so deep

invisible to all

yet constantly present within me

each breath i take

a reminder of that night

each heartbeat

a drum of sorrow

i try to bury the pain

but it claws its way back to the surface

a ghost that refuses to be exorcised

i am a vessel of silent screams

my voice stolen by your actions

but still

i refuse to be defeated

i am stronger than the scars you left behind

i will rise from the ashes

and rebuild myself anew

## WEARY

in this space

weariness takes on a form unrelated to mere sleep;

it's an exhaustion woven into the fabric of interactions

shaped by the presence of those surrounding me

# MENDED

i make no apologies

for how i chose to mend

what you shattered

my way of stitching

the cracks you left

without asking

if they hurt

## THE BITTERSWEET ODE OF HEARTBREAK

each tear that falls

a tribute to you

for only you hold the power to bruise me

black and blue

## LISTENING ARMS

you said

"i don't know how to help"

my answer is

open your ears and listen

and spread your arms wide

for when I stumble and fall

i crash like waves who have severed a storm

to feel you nearby

would soften even the hardest blow

## PAPERCUT

when it happened

it felt like a car crash—

my body

broken and bruised

a little while after

it was like tripping and grazing my knees

now

well now it's mostly okay

until

out of the blue

i get a papercut

and suddenly

the wound opens again

## THE COST OF LIBERATION

i wanted to leave

but as soon as i opened my mouth

my lungs would buckle

i couldn't speak

it felt like i was suffocating

trapped by fear

so i lit a fire inside to set myself free

but it burned everything around me

now i'm alone

realising the price of trying to break free

## UNEARNED BURDENS

just because i can hold this pain in my heart

doesn't mean i deserve to

## SELF-LOVE STRUGGLE

yes

you can both love and hate someone at once

i feel that way about myself

every day

# IGNITED

what else was she supposed be

when all you saw was a ball of fire

ignited in her belly

you gave her two options:

find someone to share the light with

or burn alive

## THE WEIGHT OF UNFULFILLED PROMISES

brought into this world

promised vast potential

believed in it growing up

now grown

realising unfulfilled expectations

## SILENT SUFFOCATION

anxiety is knowing how to speak

but my hands betray me

tightening around my throat

no one hears my silent cries

as i suffocate in fear

shoulders heavy with the weight

of a burden i cannot release

it's all my fault

this self-inflicted torment

a prisoner of my thoughts

trapped within my mind

# LETTING GO

torn between whispered memories and the wind

a hurricane dances in wild abandon

each whirl exhales a bittersweet tale

knowing this fleeting love will soon meet its end

learning to let go is not easy indeed

for even nature mourns the loss of what was

**LISTEN**

i wasn't trying to win

the argument was never the point

all i wanted was for you

to understand

to see beyond the words

and into my heart

that was breaking

just to be heard

## ICE COLD

when they ask about you

i feel the chill

sharp as ice sliding

down my spine

numbing the warmth

that once held your name

# COMMUNICATION

i always thought if we communicated more

we could make this work

but the truth is

we were over well before there were words to share

## REFLECTION

we didn't get married

but why is it that you still took half of me when you left?

left with an emptiness that echoes your absence

a void where a piece of me once belonged

## BETRAYAL

from stars in my eyes

to a dagger in my chest

your love shifted

a celestial dream turned

into a piercing ache

a bright betrayal

# GIVE ME JUST ONE MORE HOUR

time

that intangible force guiding our lives

often feels abundant until we attempt to strip away from it all that we possess

all that we cherish

in the pursuit of material gain or transient pleasures

we risk losing sight of life's true essence – it's not about what we take

but what we give

what we nurture

what we cultivate within ourselves and around us

time

once considered merely the rhythmic beating of a heart

gains profound significance as we approach our final moments

in those breaths nearing the end

time becomes the most precious commodity

a limited resource we wish we had treated with more devotion and respect throughout our journey

# COMPANIONSHIP

your companion should enhance your life

not deplete it

staying when it hurts

is not love

## NEVER TWICE

some hearts are like old books

dog-eared and worn with use

but not every page deserves

a second chance to bruise

## THE ELEMENTS

what am i to do when water doesn't mix with fire

and i happen to be both?

caught between the calm depths and the raging flames

struggling to find harmony within myself

## NINETEEN AGAIN

the disco ball spins above
casting fractured light over my head
he didn't want me
so i find solace in the rhythm of strangers
they soothe the discord in my mind
whispering comfort through the noise
"romance is a fairy tale" he said
and in that moment
i knew i had to leave
but i found comfort living in his shadow
crying
dancing
and finally sleeping—
this is the routine of a girl whose love has died

## ETERNAL WINTER

it's time to skip past these life clichés

when my heart stopped

does it need to beat again?

the rain pours

the sun beckons through the window

how can i accept the depth of life

only to see its heights?

i miss the body aches from the change of seasons

autumn into winter

i can hear the sirens—

beat

beat

beat—

it's started again

and i'm in an eternal winter

## PAID CONVERSATIONS

"do you ever feel like you want to die?" my therapist asked her eyes filled with concern

it's not that I want to die

but I can't deny the allure of the peace that comes with being on the brink of death

the chaos and noise of the world can be overwhelming

and the idea of finding solace in silence is something my soul craves

death

however

is not a welcome visitor

it brings sadness and grief to those left behind

leaving empty spaces where love once thrived and memories that linger in the halls of time

so

no

i do not want to die

i simply long to find a way to survive

to navigate through the darkness and emerge into the light

# EMPTY BOTTLES

in the darkness of my room

i drowned my sorrows with another bottle

countless nights spent calling out your name

hoping for a different ending to this cruel game

the burn in my throat matched the pain in my heart

a desire to scream

to tell you i can't handle this anymore

but i always let you back in

just like before

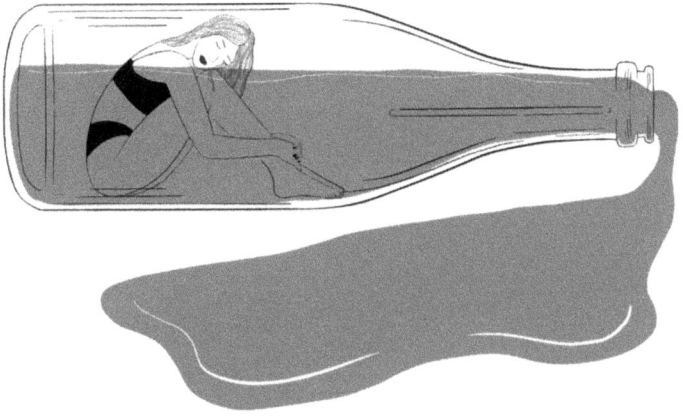

# MORE THAN A COLLECTABLE

he gathers us like shoes

adding to his collection

each one a mere accessory

to adorn his presentation

we're not meant to gather dust

in the corner of his life

we are living

breathing souls

yearning to thrive

to be valued

not discarded

to be cherished

not overlooked

for we are more than collectibles

our worth cannot be mistaken

## SHADOWED THOUGHTS

my depression is creeping in again

a shadow lurking in the corners of my mind

whispering doubts and fears

dragging me down into the depths of despair

it wraps around me like a heavy cloak

squeezing the air from my lungs

leaving me gasping for breath

lost in a maze of darkness

i try to fight back

to push the darkness away

but it's a relentless foe

always waiting for its chance to strike

so i huddle in the shadows

lost in my own thoughts

waiting for the light to break through

and chase the darkness away once more

## HEAR MY GALE

in the quiet moments

i revisit that day

when we gathered to honour your life

a promise lingered

heavy in my heart

to sing for you

one last time

but as the notes escaped my throat constricted

breath caught in the grip of grief

i faltered

unable to push through

falling short of the strength you instilled within me

how i longed to share the melody

the anthem of your life endeavours,

"i can't help falling in love with you"

a true testament to the woman you were

for you

i wish i could have found the courage

to gift you one last song

yet

in my silence please understand

each note

every melody

you're the one in my thoughts

## UNSEEN STORMS

in the midst of a storm within my soul

my mother's words echoed

gentle and wise

"take an umbrella," she softly utters

but little did she know

the rain that fell was not falling

from the skies

## PAIN AND REDEMPTION

in the darkness

i lay in bed

wide awake

haunted by that night

the memory of pain and regret

still lingers in my mind

i often think of ending it all

the thoughts of escape tempting me

but perhaps my story is not done

maybe there's a brighter ending to see

i cling to hope

fragile and faint

a flickering flame in the dark

i write my own narrative

my own fate

searching for the missing spark

so i lay in this hospital bed

restless and lost

hoping for a resolution

a sign

that my story is not yet exhaust

# THE REFLECTION

## UNBOUNDED DREAMS

imagine a world where we as women
could walk freely without fear
where our bodies are not seen as objects
but as vessels of strength and power
what could we achieve if we weren't constantly on guard?
or if we didn't have to navigate through the world
with keys between our fingers and pepper spray in our bag
always prepared for the worst to happen
we could soar to new heights
reach our fullest potential
unhindered by the weight of fear and mistrust
that has been placed upon us by society
we could build bridges instead of walls
create art that moves souls
lead with compassion and empathy
and truly make a difference in this world
so let's imagine a world where women can be free
to live
love
and thrive without constraint
where our voices are heard and respected
and our dreams know no bounds

## FADED

coffee stains on my teeth

from the cup you pour every sunday morning

you touch me

and i feel your warmth

as bright as the morning sunrise

all the pills i take

turn colours to grey

red

orange

blue—

there are things i want to say to you

# CHASING TIME

in the hustle of life

time slips by swiftly

we rush

we roam

living without restraint

choosing thrill over conformity

our wild hearts push us forward

grasping each moment tightly

before the clock ticks its final tock

## ANYTHING BUT ORDINARY

in a world that craves conformity and sameness

i find solace in the unique and the strange

the deep thinkers

the deep feelers

those who dance to their own rhythm

they are the ones who dare to question

to challenge what they are told

not afraid to dream big

or think far beyond societies mould

i am drawn to those labelled "crazy"

"weird" or "different"

for they hold a wisdom

that others often miss

they see through the darkness

yet still believe in light

their souls are old

yet timeless

guiding us through the night

if you are one of these

know that you are not alone

for i see you

i love you

and together we will make our home

## UNDERSTAFFED

i'm sorry it took six days to respond

my mind is heavily understaffed

## TOMORROWS SUN

in the chase of shadows from tomorrow's sun

we danced amidst the promise of distant dreams

leaving today as a mere bystander

neglected

now

in the quiet wake

an incomplete yesterday lingers

yet

within this lingering

lies the essence of our journey

a tale waiting to unfold

## BLOOM

trying to find love

through casual connections

is like poking dirt

expecting flowers to appear

## BEAT-UP BARINA

for an entire year, i had the same recurring dream. i found myself leaving my old primary school, wandering through the carpark, searching for my old beat-up barina. with each step, the carpark seemed to expand, making it harder to find my car.

i often pondered the significance of this dream. was my subconscious trying to tell me something? perhaps it was. during that period, i felt lost and anxious, much like i did back then. my mind kept taking me back to a place where i was bullied and trapped by hurtful people.

if this dream was a lesson, it taught me that while i cannot change the past, i can shape my future. i vowed never to surround myself with those who do not honour my heart.

i never found my car in that primary school carpark, but i did find the courage to speak up and remove negative people from my life.

# GUIDED BY WOMEN

in quiet moments

when the world fades

i find solace in the women in my life

their laughter soothes my soul

their touch heals my wounds

their love defies words

lifting me when i fall

their strength guides me through storms

with unwavering grace

each woman brings something unique

warmth

understanding

passion

though different

they make me whole

no possession or pleasure compares

to their love

a cherished treasure

## GOODBYE

release what does not hold onto you

if the connection is not mutual

there is no point in pursuing it

instead of trying to resurrect the past

let it rest

treasure the positive memories and progress when it is time to move on

## OCEAN HEART

her heart was as deep as the sea

casting tsunamis with every breath after falling apart

her emotions

unfathomable

no one could ever dive deep enough to truly know her

her soul would sever and dissipate

drifting between the atlantic and pacific

never staying in one place for too long

An Ode to the Ocean in my Heart

# TODAY'S SUNFLOWER

maybe

in another lifetime

i will be hers

close enough to touch

to feel her breath against my skin

but for now

i am bound to the shadows

loving her from afar

a silent ache that fills the empty spaces

i watch her light from a distance

a flame i can never hold

and carry this quiet longing

in the hollow of my heart

## BURNING EMBRACE

to the intensity of your heat

to the passion of your flames

in your embrace

i find peace

in your glow

i find strength

you are my fire

my light in the darkness

my constant companion in times of need

i am drawn to you like a moth to a flame

And i willingly surrender to your power

for in your burning embrace

i am reborn

renewed

and transformed

you are my fire

my salvation

and i will forever be consumed by your love

## SLOW DOWN

have you ever noticed how people tend to gravitate towards things that provide instant gratification? whether it's a 15-minute meal, a hot coffee, an audiobook, or store-bought flowers, we often seek convenience in our fast-paced lives.

but have you truly experienced the satisfaction of taking the time to prepare a meal from scratch? marinating ingredients, selecting fresh produce and cooking a homemade dinner that's makes the ones you love smile.

similarly, have you savoured a cup of coffee with a good book, fully immersing yourself in the moment? taking time to enjoy simple pleasures like this brings a sense of fulfillment.

and what about planting flowers from seeds, nurturing them, and witnessing them bloom? though slow, the reward of seeing life blossom is priceless.

time may seem infinite, but it's fleeting. by slowing down and appreciating life's small moments, we create lasting memories. in the end, it's these simple pleasures we cherish most.

## WHY I WRITE

poetry is a bridge between souls

a language of the heart

breaking barriers and prohibitions

connecting us from the start

it whispers secrets in the night

shouts truths in the day

a mirror reflecting our fears

a light showing us the way

through poetry

we find solace

in knowing we're not alone

our emotions laid bare on the page

a connection that's all our own

let your words flow freely

express what's in your core

for poetry is connection

and it's a power we can't ignore

# NEURODIVERGENT

chaos and creativity

intertwined companions

in a world where focus remains elusive

impulsivity reigns

a force uncontained

guiding a journey without a set course

my thoughts sway in unpredictable patterns

like leaves tossed by the wind

ideas flare and fade

transient and bright

as i attempt to navigate the chaos in my mind

through the twists and turns of imagination

i find solace in the unpredictability

creativity flourishes amidst the turmoil

discovering beauty in this unexpected ride

balancing order and disorder is a constant challenge

within the labyrinth of my mind's unrest

yet

amidst this blend of chaos and creativity

i find that they are both

eternal friends

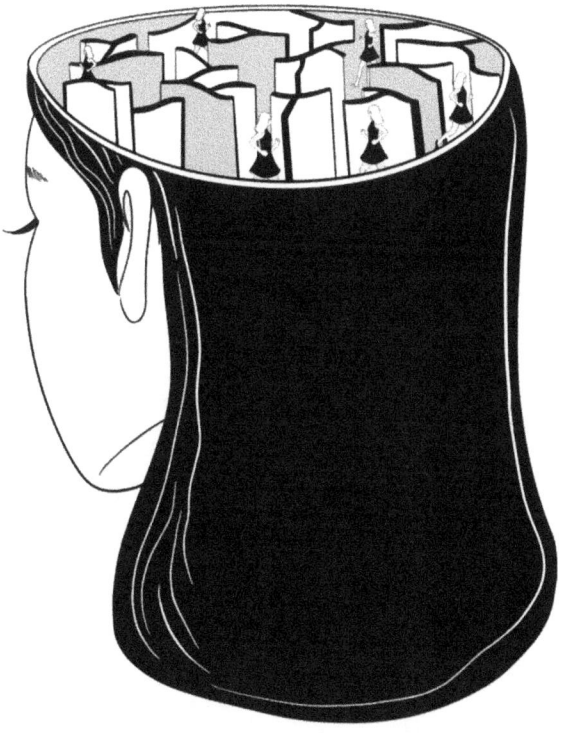

# THE LOVE

## SHADOW

it's your wet nose kisses in the morning

that gets me out of bed even on the darkest days

the way your eyes light up when i pick up a ball

sparks a light in my heart

a flicker of joy

as you lean against my leg

you somehow know

my heart is trembling

yet you offer comfort

you're like a missing limb from my body

found at last

completing me

my boy shadow

you are every star in my universe

guiding me through every night with unwavering love

# WAITING ON SUNRISE

your absence lingers like the stars yearning for the return of the sun

their light dimmed by the vast expanse of dawn

longing for the warmth that once filled their celestial embrace

## DESIRES

"and what do you desire most?"

i crave a love that engulfs me

each morning

it's my first thought

and every night

it's what i seek

feeding my soul

the love i keep

## COSMIC DANCE

our atoms

entwined like dancers in the cosmos

fused with purpose

an alchemy of connection

a fiery project

ablaze with passion's glow

in this union

we discover love's perfection

## LOCK AND KEY

unlock your destiny's doors

remember

you are the master key

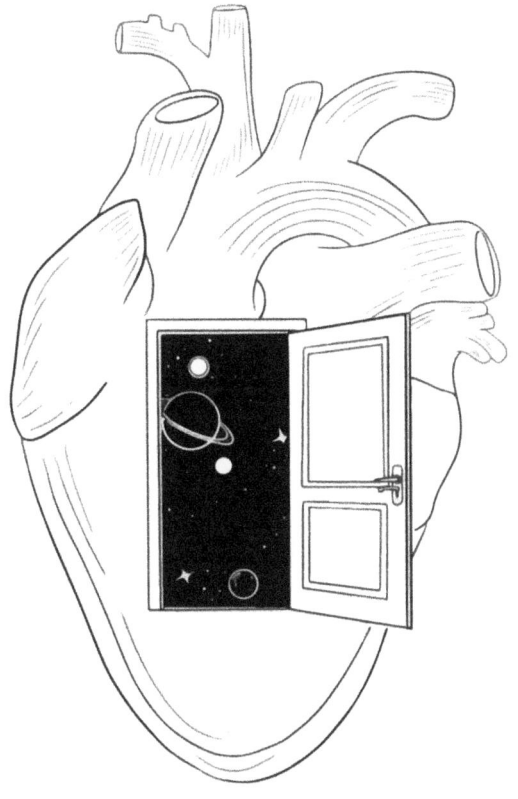

## YOU

i fell for your mind before anything else

before the way you smiled or the sound of your voice

it was in the depths of your thoughts

where i found a connection that left me no choice

your words danced like poetry in my head

creating a symphony of emotions within

i was captivated by the depth of your intellect

and the way you saw the world through eyes so keen

you challenged my beliefs and expanded my views

pushing me to grow and evolve each day

i found solace in our conversations

a safe haven where my heart could freely sway

it wasn't just your physical beauty that drew me in

but the brilliance and passion that ignited a fire

i fell for your mind

for it was a treasure trove

of wisdom

curiosity

and endless desire

so here i am

captured by the magic of your thoughts

grateful for the bond we share

for i fell for your mind before anything else

and it's there that my love will forever reside

## LOVE CONQUERS ALL

always choose love over fear

love is a powerful force that surpasses fear in every way

it's innate

coming from deep within us

while fear often stems from external influences

love is illogical and unexplainable; it simply exists

choosing love over fear is an act of courage

fear may seem monstrous

with multiple heads

but it's ultimately an illusion

love however

is real and tangible

i urge you

dear one

to always choose love

love is always the answer

## GRANDPARENTS

growing up

i always knew you would be there

i never doubted you'd be in the front row

watching me dance

i never imagined a day where you wouldn't be

the one applauding me

or picking me up when i fall

i would do anything to hear your laugh once more

or to hear you say you love me

even on my darkest days

growing up

we don't realise what little time we have

with the ones we love most

until we're holding their hand in a hospital

saying our final goodbyes

wishing they could see us dance

    just

        one

            more

                time

An Ode to the Ocean in my Heart

## WILDFLOWER

i'm the type of girl

who falls in love with flowers

the wild ones that were not planted with purpose

those that fought through the wind

yet still managed to bloom in multicolours

## TO MY MOTHER

you were dealt a hand that could never be challenged by another

yet you maintained a poker face so strong that no one could see what was truly hidden behind your hands

you are one of the strongest women i know

and i aspire to possess even a fraction of your strength

i hope that one day you will allow yourself to release the deck of cards held close to your chest

so that you can finally begin to heal from the childhood you did not deserve

## TO MY FATHER

you were the unexpected surprise that your parents never knew they needed

while some moved afar

some stole

and deceived

your intentions were always pure

you consistently chose to take the high road

even though you were the youngest

your actions are everything i aspire to be

i hope you realise in your heart that you were the child who made your parents most proud

you were the best

unexpected surprise

that could have ever been imagined

## TO MY BROTHER

in our shared childhood

i fought fiercely to keep you safe

through trials too heavy for tender souls to bear alone

you

the sensitive one

and i

the elder sibling entrusted with your care

as our mother battled illness

i held you close

a surrogate guardian in her absence

and in our father's fear

i sought to fill the void

nurturing your heart with love and care

know this

dear brother

in life's storms

i'll stand by your side

as friend

a protector

and steadfast companion

bound by the unbreakable tie of siblinghood

## TO MY BEST FRIEND

in the journey known as life
you've been my rock
standing by me through every stumble and fall
even when i've veered far off course
through thick and thin
you've stayed true
choosing me even in moments where i have hurt you the most
they say true friendship is tested in adversity
and you've embraced this with unwavering commitment
you've wiped away my tears in the quiet of my home
amidst the joyous chaos of festivals
and in the sterile silence of hospital walls
all within my darkest moments
you
my dearest daisy
are more than a friend
you're the embodiment of unconditional love
lifting me when I couldn't lift myself
granting me the courage to face tomorrow
your presence is a beacon of light
guiding me through life's darkest nights
you're not just my best friend
but my soulmate
the one i know i can conquer anything with
by my side
always

## MY ENTIRE WORLD

my shadow

he's the star that shines brightest

on days when the world trembles

grounding my feet

clearing my mind

he's the reason i wake with purpose

i throw the covers off each morning because i know he is the one beside me

my shadow is my world

nothing on this planet could ever

ever

mean more to me than him


- my soulmate is my dog.

# JOURNEY THROUGH GENERATIONS

while my hands are ice cold

she pours a cup of tea

chasing the chill from my fingertips

oh

how i hope this warmth lasts

my mother's love stems from a broken past

a history i have not lived

yet carry within me all the same

she cultivates a garden of abundance

to heal the heart of her inner child

and in return

it mends mine

in ways i have no words for

i long to create the magic she weaves

to nurture a world with her boundless love

## LOVE SPEAKS IN SILENCE

"how do you know if it's love?"

"maybe it's when you feel something so deep

words slip away

and only the silence speaks"

## SUNDAY AFTERNOONS

i crave a partner who envisions embarking on every adventure life offers

yet finds solace in the quiet stillness of rainy sunday afternoons

where time lingers lazily

cocooned in the comfort of shared silence

## HER

every time she glances my way, my stomach lodges itself in my throat, a silent barricade against the urge to pull her close and taste her breath.

when she stands near, a hush falls over the world, and my mind, a restless wanderer, traces the contours beneath her clothes, weaving fantasies from shadows and silk.

i never dreamed my heart could yearn so fervently, but desire knows no boundaries, and the heart, in its relentless pursuit, craves what it wants the most.

# THE ONE, AGAIN

when you begin to love someone new

you may find yourself chuckling at the unpredictable nature of love

remember when you were convinced that your previous partner was "the one"?

and yet

here you are

in the process of redefining what it means to be "the one" all over again

love has a way of surprising us and challenging our preconceived notions

## PLEASURE WITHOUT YOU

staying with you

i learned something vital:

how to attend to my own needs

i no longer need a man's hands to make me feel complete

to validate my worth

i've discovered i don't need to offer my body

sacrificing my desires for someone else's satisfaction

i've found the secrets to make my own heart race

to send shivers down my spine

to make my legs tremble with pleasure

i know the rhythms of my body

the language it speaks

and i can fulfill its desires

i don't need anyone to guide me to ecstasy

to make me sweat and pulse with life

my own two hands hold the key

my own touch

my own love

i am enough for myself

## INNER LONGING

we crave a greater love

not solely from others

but from the depths within ourselves

a love that fills the hollow spaces

we keep hidden

amongst each other

we search for something lasting

a bond that holds us steady

when the world frays at the edges

we long to be seen

not just by others

but by our own eyes

to find peace in our own presence

and strength in the quiet company

of souls reaching out

seeking

together

a love that's whole

## SILENT MOMENTS

before our lips met

before our hands entwined

i loved you silently

in quiet moments

in stolen glances

a bond whispered of eternity

a love felt deep within

pure and destined

before our love story begins

## SUNDAY MORNINGS

in the soft glow of sunday morning light
i wish for more moments waking next to you
the gentle rise and fall of your chest
the warmth of your skin against mine
a fleeting glimpse of paradise in your eyes
time suspended
lost in our own little world
where the worries of the week fade away
and all that matters is this moment
this simple
perfect moment
where i am with you
and nothing else exists

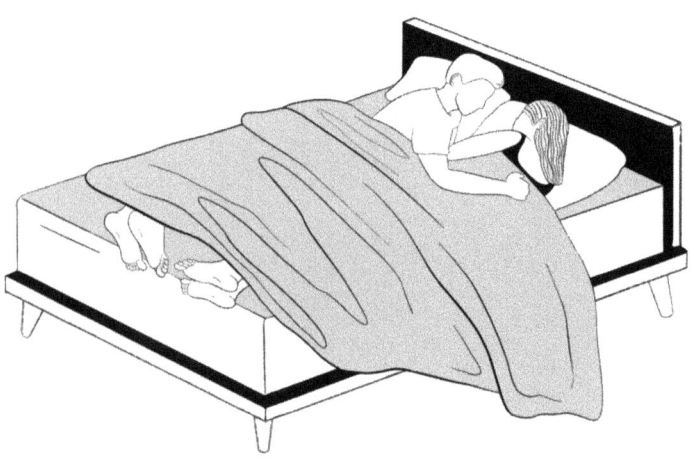

## HOLD ON

find someone who can understand your silence

read the sadness in your eyes

and remind you of your worth

look for someone who brings out your playful side

encourages you to chase your dreams

and makes you feel loved and respected

seek out someone who turns everyday moments into adventures

can make you laugh

and inspires you to be the best version of yourself

find someone you can grow and learn with

be vulnerable with

and who prioritises you

if you find that special person

cherish them and keep them by your side

## YOUR LIGHTHOUSE

in your darkest despair

i'll be the guiding light

through stormy seas of your hardest days

i'll be the anchor

holding you steady

release your fears and doubts

embrace the power within

in your feelings lies the beauty of humanity

and the strength to conquer any obstacle

feel deeply

knowing i'm always here

to hold you close and lift you high

my love knows no bounds

## LOVES MEASURE

time is an ocean

vast and endless

but for the ones we love

we only hold a handful of water

## YOUR GAZE

under a sky of stars

his gaze was always on me

## WET DREAM

when your gaze finds me

it's like a wet dream

drifting among the stars

a touch of the unreal

wrapped in the night sky's

quiet desire

## OUT OF THE DARK

in shadows deep

i once dwelled

lost in doubt

my soul's shell

now i rise

spirit sparked

loving myself out of the dark

tender grace lights my way

embracing light each day

with each heartbeat

a new start

loving myself out of the dark

no longer bound by fear

i dance with joy

release pain

in quiet moments

simply me

loving myself out of the dark

reclaiming worth

power

voice

rising from past mistakes

forgiving

loving every part

walking toward brighter days

loving myself out of the dark

# THE HEALING

## MIND IN THE COSMOS

in the vast expanse of my mind
i wander
untethered from the constraints of your words
whispers echo through the cosmic void
twinkling like stars in the boundless night
seeking moments of clarity
to form a response pure and right
lost in a labyrinth of thoughts and dreams
i search for meaning in this tangled web
emotions ebb and flow like tides
crashing against my soul's shores
yearning for understanding
to unravel unfolding mysteries
in this realm of endless possibilities
i find solace in surrounding chaos
a symphony of voices harmonises
creating a melody resonating deep within
navigating this maze of uncertainty
i lose myself in clouds of contemplation

## LET LOVE IN

on the days when the echoes of your trauma drown out the whispers of love

it's crucial to remind yourself that your worth transcends the pain you've endured

you are not defined by your scars or the wounds inflicted upon you

instead

you are resilient

being capable of healing and growth beyond the limitations of past suffering

embrace the strength within you

for it is greater than any darkness that may try to overshadow you

## COPING MECHANISMS

seeking refuge in darkness

you found solace in unhealthy coping mechanisms

forgive yourself for the paths taken in the name of survival

in the midst of chaos and hardship

you were simply doing the best you could

# HEALING WITHIN

"who will listen to my cries, who will heal my hurt?"

the silence lingered

heavy and oppressive

then

a small voice within me stirred

a gentle echo from the depths of my soul

it answered

"you. you've always been the one to listen, always the one to mend. this time is no different."

## SAVING MYSELF

for all your help

i thank you

but now

it's time to save myself

no longer will i sacrifice

my own sanity

for the sake of politeness

my own well-being

for the sake of your comfort

i will no longer be held captive

by the chains of obligation

bound by invisible strings

tied to your generosity

it's time to break free

to stand tall

and walk away

from the shadows of servitude

i thank you for all you've done

but now

it's time to save myself

## RISE AGAIN

let go of yesterday and its burdens

for each sunrise holds new beginnings

embrace the possibilities of today

seize the life you were meant to live

starting now

# UNSOLVED PUZZLE

sometimes

we must break ourselves

in order to leave behind

the pieces we no longer need

## THE LIGHT IN THE DARK

i know it's difficult

and it hurts like hell

your mind is a storm of relentless questions

and the pain feels like it will never end

with only darkness ahead

it feels like you won't make it through this time

tonight will be hard

and tomorrow

and maybe the night after that

but remember

you've faced this before

you have the strength within you to overcome it again

i believe in you

you will get through this

just like all the times before

you will be okay

you will

be

okay

## SHE TRIED

she tried to write

she tried to paint

she tried to smile through the pain

she tried

and that is truly what matters

## EMBRACE IMPERFECTION

in the shadows of my flaws

i find my strength

no need for your mending touch

just your gentle embrace

let me be

in all my imperfect glory

for i am not a puzzle to solve

but a soul to be loved

each scar a chapter

each quirk a verse

weaving the tapestry of me

in all my messy beauty

don't seek to alter

what makes me whole

just love me as i am

unapologetically me

# BE KIND

in the journey of life

be kind to yourself

you're doing your best with what you've been dealt

## TWENTY SEVEN

as morbid as it sounds

i always thought i would die at 27

many of the world's greatest left earth at that age

their brilliance snuffed out

leaving us in a haze

but now i understand the truth

their being should not have left earth

instead

their old self should have died

to make way for a brand-new birth

i always thought i would die at 27

but now i see the beauty in this notion

for my old life needed to wither away

in order to create a new

profound devotion

now i am reborn

a woman of strength

capable of achieving greatness beyond measure

from the depths of rock bottom

i rise again

digging my claws in and claiming my treasure

yes

i died at 27

it's true

but it's the death that gave birth to my new self

and with this understanding

i pursue

a life filled with purpose and infinite wonders

## SOLACE

when the one you shared everything with is no longer present

you may find solace in memories cherished

though they may be transient

seek comfort in the support of friends or family near

and allow yourself time to grieve

to heal

to persevere

# HER WINGS

she battled her demons and wore her scars

as the wings of an angel

# SCARS

i look at my scars and see the stories they tell

of pain

suffering

anger

and despair

i inflicted them on myself

seeking relief

but they only deepened the hurt

these scars remind me of a dark time

but also of my strength and resilience

i survived

and i am still here

i am not ashamed of my scars

they are part of me

telling my story

a testament to overcoming adversity

and to being stronger than i ever imagined

i am proud of the scars that tell my story

# EMBRACING THE STRUGGLE

the pain may never fully fade

but neither will your strength

to keep living despite it

## ME AND THE SEA

he asks about my affinity for the sea

and i explain that the soothing sound of the waves brings me peace

however

it goes beyond that

i am drawn to the sea because

i believe it listens to me as well

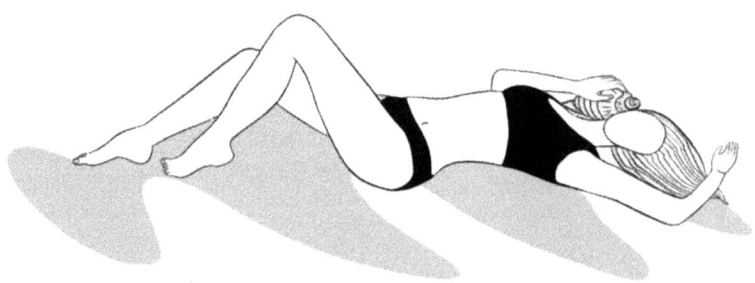

## TAKE TIME

it's okay to disappear until you find yourself again

sometimes

the journey inward is the only way to rediscover the essence of who you are

## MY TURN

this time

it's personal

this is an apology to myself

this comeback is for me

# SWIM

after that night

i was sinking to the bottom of the ocean

somehow

my lungs filled with air

giving me the strength to rise in the depths where i was drowning

it's time to fight

to swim

it's time to save yourself

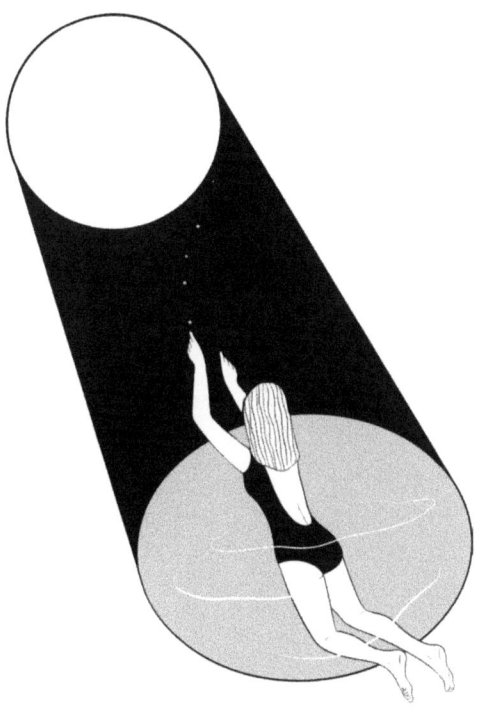

## LET IT BE

in the depths of despair

let it hurt

for pain

though raw

will give birth

to strength and resilience deep in the soul

allowing wounds to mend and make us whole

like a wound that bleeds

let it flow

let every drop release the sorrow

for in bleeding out

we find release

a cleansing of heartache

a sense of peace

but as time passes by

let it heal

let the scars form

a testament

surreal

for in healing lies the power to grow

to learn from the past

and wisdom bestow

and when the time is right

let it go

release the burdens that weigh us low

for liberation lies in shedding the pain

embracing new chapters with hope to attain

so

let it hurt

let it bleed

let it heal

and in the end

remember to reveal

that the human spirit emerges stronger still

when we let it go

and allow our hearts to fill

# THE GROWING

## RESTLESS WATERS

within my heart

an ocean stirs

a tumultuous sea of emotions and fears

waves of joy and sorrow clash and collide

as i navigate the turbulent tide

deep beneath the surface lies a mystery

a hidden world of thoughts and memories

whispers of the past echo in the dark

haunting me like a restless shark

but amidst the chaos

there is peace

a calmness that brings me sweet release

i dive deep into the depths of my soul

exploring the mysteries that make me whole

within my heart

an ocean stirs

a vast expanse of emotions that blurs

i ride the waves of uncertainty and doubt

knowing that within

i will always find my route

## SOWING SEEDS OF CHANGE

to nurture gardens, we become gardeners

to embody love, we must embrace it

to enact change, we must forge our path

to foster connection, we extend our reach

to find our place, we stand firm

to create a home, we nurture it

to love ourselves fully, we honour those we admire

to make a difference in the world

we must start by making a difference in our own lives

# MY SOULS GUARDIAN

along life's path

growth is continuous

but there's a point where you become the caretaker of your own soul

looking back

you wish to reassure past versions of yourself

but understand that in the future

you'll long to do the same

## SOFTNESS IN STRENGTH

in my quest for resilience and strength

i'm learning that my softness is not a sign of weakness

# BEYOND THE HOSPITAL BED

i've seen the other side

it's dark

quiet

yet peaceful

awakening in a hospital bed was like waking to my worst nightmare

bright

loud

sorrow filling the room

scratchy sheets

rough as the memories from last night

how do i soften this blow?

i search for solace in the stillness of the night

in the gentle touch of a loved one

in the warmth of a comforting embrace

i find peace

on the other side of pain

i find hope

in the quiet moments of reflection

i find strength

to face the challenges ahead

i've seen the other side

and i'm still standing

stronger

braver

ready to face whatever comes next

# FLAME IN THE NIGHT

in my life's darkest room

shadows move

sharp yet silent

echoes whisper in the dark air

weight of breath heavy with doubt

but even here

in deep despair

i find strength

a flicker of hope

a flame within

yearning to shine

# BEYOND MY TWENTIES

in my dreams

i envision the woman i strive to become

shedding the chaos of my tumultuous twenties

i eagerly anticipate the confidence and resilience that lie ahead

knowing that my younger self will one day be grateful for the journey i have embarked upon

# EMBRACING THE JOURNEY

trust that time remains for you to grow into the person you aspire to be

there is still space in your journey for transformation

for becoming your true self

**GROWING**

growth takes to forms:

a flower in full bloom

reaching for the sun

or a flower

clinging to its last petal

each fighting

to be seen

## CLOSED EYES

as i close my eyes

i remind myself i am still young

still navigating the labyrinth of learning

the universe stretches infinitely

and so

too

do i

a boundless expanse of becoming

forever unfolding

forever new

# DAWN OF COURAGE

in the quiet dawn

before the world awakes

you rise from the shadows of your pain

a weary soul

longing for rest

but you summon the strength to face another day

through the darkness that clouds your mind

you cling to hope

a flickering flame

courage beating in your heart

pushing through the obstacles that stand in your way

you are a warrior

fierce and bold

a fighter in the face of despair

never giving up

even when all seems lost

your resilience a testament to your strength

it's brave to keep going

when the road is rough

to face the uncertainties with a steadfast resolve

so hold your head high

my dear

for you are a beacon of light in a world full of shadows

## STAY

a simple truth: what's yours will find you

love freely

without need to possess or control

let connections flow

unbound by attachment

let your heart embrace what stirs your soul

trust in me

trust in yourself —

what's meant to stay

will stay

you'll never lose what's truly yours

please

always remember that

## WISE CHOICES

life is tough already

don't make it harder

by putting all of your eggs

into the wrong basket

## SPARK IN THE SHADOWS

for those who have endured darkness

there is always a glimmer of light

a flicker of hope

their stories serve as a powerful reminder to persevere

even in the most challenging times

despite the depths of despair

there is always a glimmer of hope shining through

# FIND THE LIGHT

people often ask

how i decided my only way out was to end it all

they wonder why i couldn't call for help

and honestly

it took time to understand

when you're fighting for air

words don't seem like an option

all you can do is follow the light

## FRAGILE WINGS, RESILIENT SPIRIT

she was a baby bird

tiny and fragile

her spirit a delicate feather

easily shattered

every disappointment is like a storm

threatening to break her wings

yet she never lost her grace

finding strength in vulnerability

small

but within her

the power of survival and growth

like a baby bird learning to fly

## THE SEED AND THE FLAME

please remember that your words

can plant gardens filled with wildflowers

but they can also ignite bushfires

that take out entire cities

your words have the power

to reshape everything around you

so be mindful before you share your thoughts

aware of the consequences they may bring

## SEARCHING

don't search for someone to complete you;

seek someone to share your completeness with

## OK

drop the facade; it's okay not to be okay

## LIFE'S LABELS

in my mind's turmoil

a constant battle stems

between soaring heights and plunging depths

emotions whirl like sand in the wind

unpredictable

beyond my control

mania tempts with promises of conquest

while depression pulls me into darkness

caught between these extremes

i am a captive of my own mind

yet within this chaos

i find resilience

to endure

to defy confinement

bipolar

they call this journey

but i won't let it dictate my identity

embracing both light and shadow

i navigate each day

one step at a time

# BREAKING THE SILENCE

now isn't the moment for silence

nor to yield space to you

when we've known no space at all

now is our moment to be outspoken

to raise our voices as high as necessary to be noticed

## FOREVER EVOLVING

the person you're evolving into surpasses the one you once recognised

each passing day brings forth fresh narratives of courage and boldness in your journey of self-discovery

while remnants of the past may linger nearby

the clarity of the future illuminates your path

embrace this journey of self-exploration with freedom

for it leads toward a horizon brimming with limitless possibilities waiting to be unveiled

## GRIEVING TO LOVE

to live is to grieve

in grief

we find our humanity

and in humanity

we learn to love despite it all

## HOMECOMING

in our journey of growth

we shed old skins

feeling lost

but let's see this change as a return

a homecoming to our true selves

embrace the new 'us' with open arms

for we're finally safe to be who we are

# BALANCING ACT

in the battle between mind and heart

who do you choose?

in the corridors of reason

the mind stands firm

analysing

calculating

seeking clarity

yet in the depths of emotion

the heart sings

whispering desires

echoing dreams

to choose the mind is to seek order

to follow the heart is to embrace passion

so who do i choose?

perhaps both

in delicate harmony

navigating the labyrinth of life

with wisdom from the mind

and guidance from the heart

but then again

when in life can you ever have both?

# UNBREAKABLE

i am not a product of my past

but a warrior forged from its fire

it's my greatest honour to embody her strength

and embrace the journey that shaped me entire

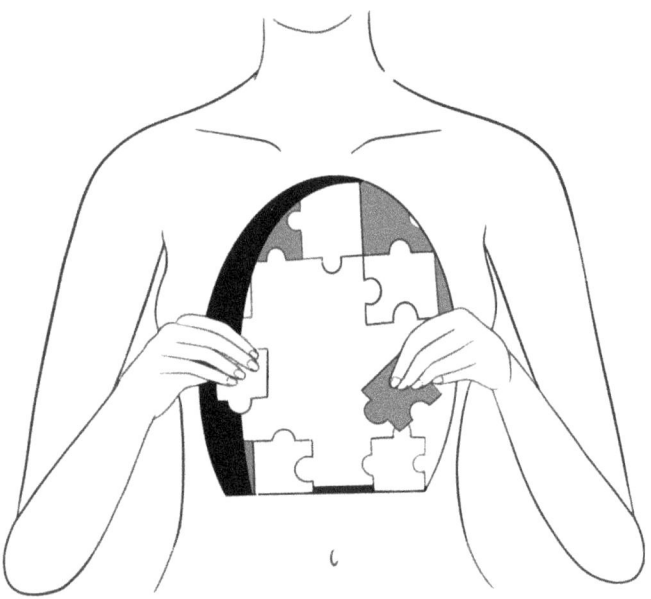

## ALONE THROUGH ADVERSITY

one thing many people don't understand

is that when you face your worst moments alone

you stop caring about who stays in your life

# RETURNING HOME

when i left you

i finally found myself

no longer tied

to your expectations

i roamed freely

through the vast unknown

discovering pieces

of my soul i had lost

in your shadow

i found my light

when i left you

i finally found myself

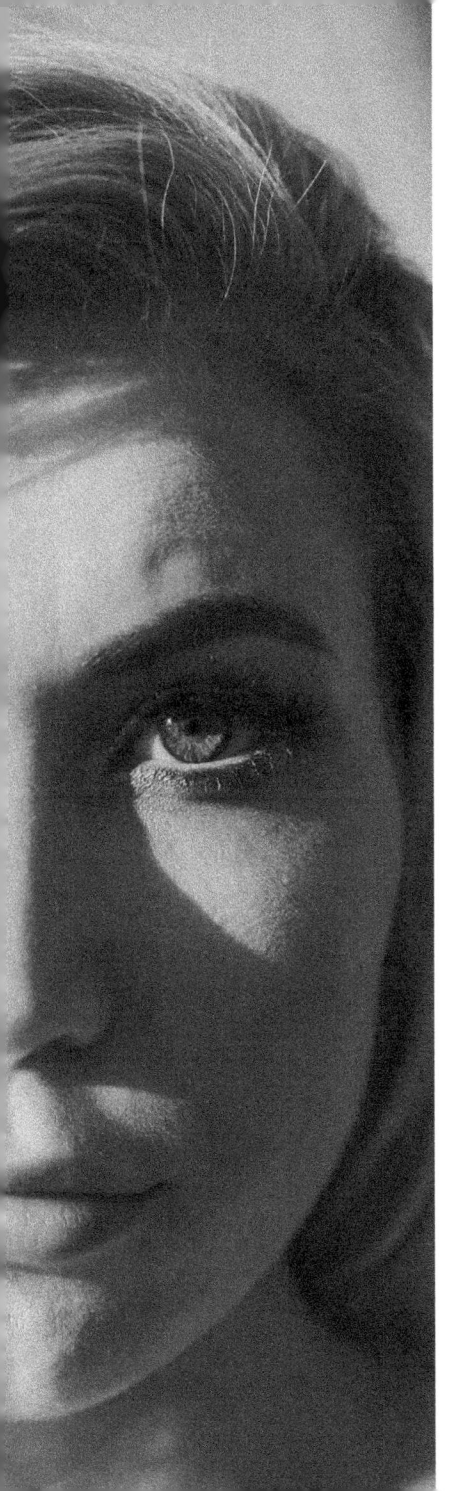

# ABOUT THE AUTHOR

Jordan Asbroek comes from South Australia's beautiful wine region, Barossa Valley. At twenty-seven, she works in marketing at a winery and has a deep passion for writing.

Writing has always been Jordan's escape. Diagnosed with depression and anxiety at sixteen, and later with bipolar disorder, she found comfort in her words. Throughout her twenties, writing was her therapy, even though she kept it mostly private.

Over the past twelve months, Jordan experienced significant losses: a seven-year relationship, her home, and the job she loved. Forced to start over, she turned to writing as her salvation. Her words became an ode to the ocean within her—vast, tumultuous, but beautiful.

Now, Jordan shares her story in her book. It's not about awards or degrees but about the raw, real experience of being a young woman in a challenging world. She hopes her words will offer comfort to others, showing they are not alone in this unpredictable journey called life.

"I am who I am today because of my parents, my brother, my best friend, and my heart and soul, my shadow. I wouldn't have made it this far without you."

**Photography**
@melissabrown_photographer

**Illustrations**
@fatimaseehar

www.ingramcontent.com/pod-product-compliance
Lightning Source LLC
Chambersburg PA
CBHW041307110526
44590CB00028B/4278